A list of your author's books
are attached in the back of this
book for your inspection.

# Understanding the Science of Creative Mind

For Discovering and Practicing
a Psychological Powerhouse within

## Lloyd E. McIlveen

*Trafford rev. 12/03/2015*

 www.trafford.com

North America & international
toll-free: 1 888 232 4444 (USA & Canada)
fax: 812 355 4082

A note from your author

"I have written this book resulting from study of philosophy, psychology, general and metaphysical sciences, nation, business and interpersonal relationships while I pursued and stumbled through the hard knocks and rewards of life.

As I progressed, both positively and negatively, I made mental and scriptural notes of what could benefit and promote human security within. This has been my contributing passion toward helping to raise the standards of the human cause.

The following scriptures are written and comprised from my personal study and observation of many years which have formed my original and exclusive text in this book.

L.E.M.

# Preface

Maybe sometime in the distant future everyone will know how to manage their minds and bodies so they will act and react in a manner where they will blend in compatibly with others and have everything they want. Fantasy? For everyone now, maybe. Later? Well, we are pioneering it now.

The present time represents an era of time when everyone is racing and striving to be a step ahead of the other guys. The problem has unfolded to be habitual in nature.

While humanity races and stumbles over one another as they did in the goldrush days and wanting as much or more of everything they can handle, they tend to ignore their senses of consciousness awareness almost as a trade-in for any gain they can acquire in a short period of time.

Specializing in all fields of endeavor is becoming more popular by the year and seems to keep more people busy so they can spend more money to acquire more things and people to live with, but are they accomplishing anything meaningful within themselves or are they just running the rat race?

Acquiring anything is fine. It's a way of life now more than ever. What isn't so fine is the manner in which people struggle to get what they want. Time goes by so fast and they are still struggling. People will do almost anything to get what they want and in so many cases they run into what seem endless problems in the process.

Most of humanity has fallen into a trap of do this to get that with hardly ever realizing learning a craft or profession for work in life is necessary, but learning how to prepare one's consciousness within for blending in and adapting to or with any situation where harmony is needed has to be a prerequisite for any encounter where success of acquiring anything is desired.

The prerequisite of mind and body consciousness awareness and control that allows one to maintain an independently chosen and stable frame of mind is what these texts are about.

The independence, attitude, self-control, health and desire to be successful within are articulated in the chapters. The results of the study will help allow one to realize and capture an excitement of being the person and character that one wants to be. The reader will also gain more understanding of what one really wants or doesn't want out of life.

The philosophy of mind control over the self is designed to help sort out mixed or vacillating anxieties and create, through the efforts of the individual, a dependable platform of useable consciousness so it doesn't just exist with no creative or constructive purpose than what others expect.

The general purpose of this study is to offer the reader a chance to experience an opportunity of gaining mind control over the entire self for creating and maintaining a strong and stable entity that will satisfy the self and be a profound influence to others.

It's about discovering a psychological powerhouse within.

# Contents

Chapter 1:  Self-control or be controlled ...................... 1

Chapter 2:  Self-acceptance and social recognition ..... 11

Chapter 3:  Directing the body and mind ................... 19

Chapter 4:  Living in self-harmony ........................... 35

Chapter 5:  Support for maximum health ................... 45

Chapter 6:  Maintaining normal energy or better ........ 55

Chapter 7:  Gaining the power of self-control ............. 65

Chapter 8:  The cost and rewards of destiny .............. 75

Chapter 9:  An attitude of how everything
            is available ............................................... 85

Chapter 10: How love is experienced or shared ........... 94

Chapter 11: Manifesting and spreading
            good or bad spirit .................................... 106

Chapter 12: Resolving the way and
            focusing on programming ...................... 122

## Chapter 1

---

# Self-control or be controlled

Life has its great moments as well as its pains and disappointments. That's the realism of life. The dreams and fantasies beside the great moments may not always fall into place possibly because of expecting them to happen without any exceptional effort. That is to say, while striving to acquire what is abnormally achievable, they also have their limitations with the greater majority of people. That is an undocumented rule one can depend on dictated by the math of odds in percentages such as fifty/fifty, sixty/forty etc. based on knowledge of past experience.

Want great things for the self? They can and will happen with desire and knowing what one wants.

That has to be arrived at first; more favorably with a passionately "strong" desire. If it's weak, the greatness of it may not unfold as in the wishful manner that was originally desired.

Accepting responsibility for the self and practicing it daily is a necessary and spiritual philosophy needed for acquiring great things. The greatest of all acquirements is that which begins within the self. The greatest of all self-acquirements is the confidence gained in realizing all other acquirements will fall into place with that basis of confidence that drives the desire for accomplishing any task or ambition. It all begins and perpetuates "within" the self.

Living beings have somehow been designed with amazing abilities by whatever our maker is. There are similarities to the making of the automobile by mankind with everything needed to function properly. Both man and the auto have limits in their functioning.

Flying a car is unreasonable to expect. By the same token of rationale, it is humanly unreasonable to expect living beings to accomplish anything beyond their scope of life's design as, for instance, extending a thought to another city or country with a very low current amperage of the human mind. Anything travelling electrically requires a certain amount of amperes to move it. Living beings do not possess that type of energy. They only possess electrical energy sufficient enough to sustain their human existence.

The electrical energy and mental capacity in controlling the human system has apparently been designed only to exceed conventional capacity through the growth and evolution of the species with the passage of time. If we humans expect or believe there is more capacity in our mental electricity beyond the design of life at the present time, we may experience some surprises in our overindulging expectations. Spiritual believing is very profound, but facts of physics are also difficult to disprove.

Sure, the "possibility" exists these very small currents "may" travel in longer distances beyond the body, but controlling the route of those frequencies would be a nebulous nightmare to say the least.

Calculated appearances indicate the design of life is where its capacity in growth increments runs parallel with or as a result of evolutionary tendencies and unfolds naturally with the passage of time or is an entity humans believe created and controls the universe; whatever one's choice may be.

Controlling the self is actually much easier than even attempting to control others than the self. Why and how? Everyday we tell ourselves what to do every minute of those days and think nothing of it being the orders from the headquarters of our minds as a result of moment to moment impulses of desire. Being aware of that wonderful potency of power within can and/or will inspire us to expand that control of the self because that's exactly what it is. It's just a matter of gathering a few ideas and programming the mind of which will be delt with as we progress through the chapters.

The obvious design of life has allowed us to have that complete control over ourselves even when things get rough. That's what these scripts are about. We are either controlled by others or by ourselves as disturbing as that may seem. Let's take our pick.

The design of life is a norm or average of how we all exist. It is proof of what our limitations are by our smooth or awkward actions. Our scope is one of our design limitations. That means we can only believe to a given extent. It seems instinctual for our human species to push our designed capacities of growth as far as possible before time permits more flexibility in that area of growth.

We were given these instincts and desires to acquire and keep what we acquire, okay? That means we "can" acquire that complete control over ourselves and keep it. That is achieved when we become aware of having the "tools" to work with from the design of life. They are available for the asking, believing and qualifying similar to that of an apprentice starting a career in a trade. How? It's a process of searching, some studying, a program of believing and practice.

The "tools" of acquiring are earned by as #1, deciding what the "self" needs and wants while realizing these tools never ware out.

The next useable tool is acquired by making inquiries (however) of what are needed by the self and knowledgeable people for fulfilling those preferences, needs and wants.

The stronger the desire for what is wanted from the self and others, the more one will acquire new awareness. It happens almost mystically. One thing will lead to another in the process of acquiring more knowledge for developing self-control. Then it becomes a way of life and an integral part of the self. Thereof and thereafter, confidence in various acquirements are built in and will be permanently maintained through practicing effort similar to that of how a doctor "practices."

All these tools to acquire and share are a matter of intellectual growth that begins exclusively within the self. When they mature through broadening perception and practice, they will branch out and add toward mingling with other people, possibly business and maybe even other nations who exchange views, ideas, skills and materials. It all starts with one decision; what one needs and wants. Effort put out is a great companion.

All good things happen within the self and with others by understanding what is wanted; not to control others, but to secure a reasonable control over the self. While practicing that self-control by exercising needed and applicable decisions, self-esteem is also built and adds toward increased confidence. There is close to almost nothing more rewarding than the growth of self-acquired confidence. That growth is excitingly inspirational with its acquired development, maturity, knowledge and social value that maintains an abundance of life's rewards. It will all unfold as the "real" things in life do when one can say, "I choose to maintain complete control over my entity while tuning in to my desires and aspirations within the scope of what I have been given through the design of life." This is profound programming and as mentioned, will be dealt with later in programming sections ahead.

Obviously, the "design of life" is what we see, hear, smell and feel which is interpretable as "real" in a similar manner of, for instance, designers jeans. Both jeans and humans appear designed for certain purposes. Jeans are smart pants, but only have a little control over the wearer. Appearances are; the design of life had a little more thought put into it. We will be forever rewarded (long run in life, that is) in respecting that design with its vast possibilities, but never to be forgotten limits. Moderation, patience, acquired belief, acquired confidence and sincere willingness to practice rationality within the self and with others will serve as useful "tools" in building and maintaining desirable control over the self. That self-control will serve as a good example to others.

Preventing involuntary exploitation will be an automatic result and developing consciousness asset of building self-control. When that concept carrys forward and is continuously realized, the individual will become less dependent on others and more emotionally stable while also developing more self-esteem which adds toward confidence and stability.

Only the ill at heart, dejected and various unfortunate victims of circumstances appear vulnerable to control of dominant and opportunistic personalities and/or organizations. If nothing else, gaining awareness of self-control "will" change or turn the course of dependence, victimization and insecurity into self control, self-sufficiency and further successes rendered from those efforts of accomplishment. Give it a whirl. Nothing will be lost from this effort and much more confidence, emotional stability and self-control will be gained to say the least.

Chapter 2

# Self-acceptance and social recognition

What could be better after suffering a debilitating and painful physical and emotional illness than enjoying a freedom from those miseries and move on to a future of vibrant and unyielding health? Most people would probably say nothing would beat that. That's one manner of appreciating good health that builds self-acceptance.

However, we don't have to suffer to be humble, thankful and appreciate the finer things within. We can cross over the bridges of misery and sacrifice by realizing good health is part of the design of life. When that health is abused by allowing the self-detrimental luxuries as unnatural substances, unfocused neurosis, excessive self-centeredness, greed and other eccentricities, the health that would ordinarily be appreciated and sustained may falter to as much as a terminal condition. That detriment can be avoided, detoured or made to cease in its existence.

Self-inflicted disease is any noncontagious illnesses such as headaches, backaches, joint aches, emphysema, stress, smoking diseases, improper digestion, paranoia, some cancers, most coronary occlusions, ills of toxic and nonnutritional consumption and other distresses propagated by and allowed to exist in the body through procrastination.

One of the biggest battles in overcoming those or any other self-inflicted disease is moving psychologically away from blaming others or things for their entry into our lives.

Giant strides of eliminating or at least offsetting these mentioned ills have been accomplished through the use of mental awareness, vocal suggestion (programming, self-hypnosis, praying etc.), proper diet, exercise and most of all a solid, sincere, bonding, but flexible belief of what we say will happen within and "will" happen in time which are equal to how much belief and effort is exercised utilizing the power and direction of mind control learned. There is no limit to its potential.

If the illness occurs suddenly, the "odds" are it will disappear in much the same time, give or take. If it's a sudden injury and not a terminal condition, nature will require more time in the healing process.

Other than sudden ills or injuries, most if not all of the common ills can be directed toward an improving course of overcoming or offsetting those ills, aside from possible professional help, by the practice of directed suggestions from the developed power of mind which changes those courses of ills with a never ending belief from whatever source one chooses and there are many as we become aware of them.

When one becomes aware these choices of mind are available, one can with patience, change the course of progress so it will occur in a manner relative to that of a rolling ball of snow. It can increase depending on the individual's strength of belief, its efforts and determination along with some assistance from nature.

Jesus, the teacher with the power of human belief, proved the power of belief and its practices could heal and it is being practiced to this day whether it is in a conventionally spiritual manner, a higher consciousness or metaphysical manner or a manner of being responsible for a destiny of self-acceptance and self-control.

The power of belief is universal and can be utilized by all in any form. The only limits or restrictions on belief for humans are those of human's contriving. The design of life undoubtedly has "some" form of limits. The human question is about our perception of what those limits are. The design of life will probably take care of that.

Meanwhile, let us continue to strive in our efforts to stabilize our mental and emotional capacity and direction toward self-acceptance which builds self-esteem and confidence in any field of our choice. The power of belief "does" fit into it all. This particular chapter stabilizes our capacities pertaining mostly to creating and maintaining self-acceptance where it prepares one for any of life's encounters.

This chapter is also about progressing in every way where one can be enthusiastic and creative for accepting the self. That self won't be accepted as such if no improvements are made, so it's beneficial to the cause of enjoying the self to, let's say, write a list of desired objectives that will enhance or enrich one's life within. For instance, your author gains tremendous intellectual satisfaction along with emotional stability in writing books while, of course, practicing what is written wherever applicable. Practicing what is preached increases emotional stability, confidence and belief in the self. This is all within. It has nothing to do with anything outside the body and mind. This is where one gains happiness, contentment and self-assurance; all within, generally speaking. Granted, there are other theories, beliefs and methods of approach. This is just one of them and it works fine.

Remember the ball of snow as these virtuous aspects are accomplished. Success builds on success while confident grows. As it grows, so does the well feeling of the self. As that well feeling increases with its support of suggestion, programming and belief, so does the feeling of self-acceptance. The progress, as usual, will unfold with time, patience and determination.

The rewards of self-acceptance can supercede as self-power over "any" outside influence of others while remaining open and flexible. When that is comfortably accomplished, that self-power acquired can be utilized toward confidently blending in almost any social situation. That means there will be a close to total acceptance in, again, almost any social scene where communicating and relating with others is on the agenda. This is important to keep in the forefront of consciousness especially in view, as a reminder, the world of people is closing in on us and almost everything we do includes necessary harmony in relating with others. Good relating, equals good results. Bad relating equals—well, may be not so good relating.

Awareness must be gathered where "social" means engaging with others somehow and exists with the overwhelming majority. In view of accepting that as reasonably true, improving the ability to relate better to others for improved compatibility seems more desirable than presenting conflict and mediocre manners of relating with others; especially when one can realize improving a relationship within the self "will" automatically improve relationships with others regardless of who they are. That is as close to a more recently accepted poll on the subject.

There is a relative combination of improving self-acceptance, belief in the self and self-confidence that enhances, improves and when constantly maintained; perpetuates healthy consciousness and relationships with others. One helps the other.

Believe the following if nothing else: All improvements developed within the self are similar to a column of numbers. The more numbers added, the larger the sum becomes. If one can believe there is more strength in numbers, this theory does apply. More numbers allow more options as in money, people, ideas and different available caring. Amounts of improvements in the self are the same. More improvements will be equal to gaining plenty of everything depending on the amount of those self developed improvements. There is a plentiful amount of numbers available and with moderation applied, the sky is the limit or thereabout.

Chapter 3

# Directing the body and mind

Some contagious diseases can be resisted and overcome when one has a strong immune system or is immune to a specific virus because of possessing certain antibodies. It is best not to assume or rely on that being the case though. There may be a rude surprise in store.

The medical approach is best for the masses of people of whom are unfamiliar or untrained to deal with a natural or wholistic approach of healing or curing. Otherwise, dealing with mind and body healing or curing has many options in this day of raising consciousness to higher levels than ever. The fact is, many of us are reviewing somewhat outdated beliefs where deity of some nature is directing and controlling everything and everybody on Earth; even the illnesses. Read your author's "Evaluating Outdated Beliefs" for more insight on the subject of believing. An extenuated version published of "Spiritual Transformation" follows later. Also, many people are standing on the fence with, assumingly, access to both sides of believing. Is it having access to both sides or is it fear of either side?

Well, the fence people are very dependent on going to medical doctors with their down to earth scientific methods and turn right around and go to church seeking religious relief. They say it's "just in case we might be wrong." What kind of belief is that? That isn't holy and it certainly isn't a self-sustaining and secure state of dependable believing.

Jesus, whether he was a messiah or not, was a shining example of pure, simple and powerful belief. He believed in what he believed one hundred percent! There was no question in his mind. That strong, unwavering and unquestionable belief is what allowed him to influence cures of many illnesses or handicaps (as least those in the Bible).

The emphasis in these views are not particularly on a judgement of conventional religion. It is on the judgement of being hypocritically confused. These people appear to not allow themselves the luxury of expanding for what is real. They are stuck in a state of indecisiveness, apprehension and fear. They can also choose a manner of believing based on reality, but good or not, they exist in that realm of thought.

Beliefs "can" change. We all have that birthright privilege having no rules or laws attached to regulate our minds in a manner we choose whenever. Yes, we have that right along with whatever options we were given regardless of who, what or wherever they came from. Let us not dilly-dally just standing on the fence wavering in question.

We all have the birthright to think, say and be as we choose within our own minds. Just as a reminder, our minds belong to us. No one or anything can dictate anything in our minds except us! We own our minds for awhile and can regulate them just like a computer and the results will unfold exactly how we programmed them. How do we do it? Read on.

Our bodies are made of communicating and nourishing cells; millions and more of them. They are obviously put there, for and from the design of life, to serve as transferring agents, if you will. Like most all agents, they have a director that tells and guides them to perform their duties in this case of feeding and communicating. Guess who or what the directors are. Our birthright allows us to pick one of three to be the director. # 1 is the conventional view of a creator. #2 are exploiters here on Earth (there are plenty of them) and #3 is the individual (you and I). It isn't as though your author is giving out these specific options for the reader to respond to; not at all. If there are any more options, let the reader be the first to discover them and latch on to them or reject them. It's a matter of birthright choice to discover and adopt.

It just so happens, your author chooses the individual for the director and that certainly doesn't mean the individual is any more qualified to make decisions than anyone or anything else. That obstinacy would defeat the purpose of birthright privilege being the fairest and most rational method for choosing. All angles are open, but choice still awaits. No "one" person can open or close all those angles. They are just available forever.

Since we will be able to choose our method of healing when ill symptoms are experienced, your author only elaborates on the choice of the individual control over those self-inflicted ills. This may be referred to as accepting and practicing responsibility "for" self-inflicted ills.

When we think, we generally assume it's happening in our head; specifically our brain, but who bothers to analyze it any further, right? Is it just a hunk of head cheese with a bunch of thoughts? Maybe it's a substation controlled by a master computer. Well, science is working on it in their way and religion in a completely other way.

While science, religion and whoever else is taking thousands of years attempting to figure it out, let's just say our thinker thinks and like any other source of thoughts, ideas, creations and other endeavors, there is usually some kind of chain of command like the space program or the U.S. government where the brains run the show and like they say, heaven forbid, they had better do it right!

We, in our heads, don't really need all that sophisticated organizing just to make decisions. All we need to know is the brain does the thinking and instigating while the headquarters of mind dictates every function in the body. What we think when we are aware of it originates from our headquarters of mind directing all thoughts, feelings and basic functions throughout our bodies.

Sure, the subconscious is the storehouse of intellect and supply's headquarters the information contributing toward delegating all the jobs out to the entire body, but what good is all that knowledge to the body if one doesn't realize it and only lets the status quo of tendencies control the flow of cells and blood etc.?

Body cells are directed and "used" similar to the function of oil, gas and wear of the car's engine. The gas and oil is filtered to help keep the engine in top condition and it eventually wears out anyway, but the better it is maintained, the longer it lasts. Body cells "must" be mentally controlled and physically assisted with proper oral consumption and exercise etc. It's an outdated and life shortening belief where the body will take care of itself. We need to control it now more than ever. That control is administered by nourishing and training the body's cells.

None of the car's engine functioning would take place, though, without the "brains" (the electrical system) starting and directing it. The body fluids and cells are similar in their function. The headquarters of the brain is constantly sending electrical and fluidic messages to all areas of the body. It won't be necessary to describe the specific densities, electromagnetic fluctuation and P.S.I. per molecule etc. of those electric, liquids and cells, but they do exist. They are real transmitters and do function real well as such.

So, ill feeling and self-inflicted disease is created by the self by virtue of the brain's headquarters directing the electricity and fluid to all parts of the body unless someone else has complete control over that body and mind which, in most cases, is typically unlikely.

Outside the body sources can influence the way headquarters directs the body cells etc. What are those sources? They are the consumption of foods, liquids, gases, odors, heat, cold, drafts, hostility, fears, terrors, weather, contagious disease, stress, strain, allergies, smoking, alcohol, dope, sugar, salt and a host of other outside the body sources and influences. No wonder we have problems. Generally, whatever we consume by swallowing, breathing, seeing, hearing, tasting, feeling or perceiving of which influences our senses to respond and make decisions quickly or in a longer period of time are what can cause our mental headquarters to send the messages internally that makes our body cells function either normally or abnormally. That function determines specific or general health and length of life. Those internal messages are the most influential guidance toward our body's stability. The stability of the mind also reacts to the body's health.

The sources behind and problems incurred because of them are detectable, treatable and conquerable in most cases by gaining awareness of how they start and continue, then accepting and practicing methods of offsetting them such as what we are studying in this book. After all, one's body "is" one's life! One is not very well equipped to help or enjoy others, let alone the self, without a sound body "and" mind to do it!

The self is a conglomeration of cells among the organs and bones etc. The health of the cells is the health of the body and sequentially, the health of mind. It functions on a repetitious cycle until foreign matter or influential suggestion enters the body or mind. Then it can move in a different course.

Now, if foreign matter or suggestion can affect the body and mind from the outside inward, then logic dictates the mind (headquarters, that is) having the flexibility of responding to outside influence or penetration also has the flexibility and intellectual ability to either direct the cells like an army or a fleet of ships so they will be protected or fight. A stable and/or well trained headquarters can successfully organize, reorganize or rearrange its body's strategy to be stronger and more resistive too adverse influence. The immune system is a closely related tool, so to speak, to assist headquarters in making quick or ongoing decisions depending on the input and nurturing of the self or the mental or physical penetration from outside the body or mind by other human application or influence.

The strength of self-influence is contingent upon stability of the mind. Mind stability is a sum total of genetic inheritance, child rearing along with educational, peer, employment, relationship and a number of other influences that either helps to build it up or tear it down. It can grow healthier and stronger or it can shrink and shrivel depending on how the self either guides it or allows it to happen by others or happenstance.

By the same token, when the self gains enough awareness of all these said possibilities, the self can begin to apply methods of suggestion and belief as mentioned and will be described further in the chapters ahead. Then one can practice while learning. When ill symptoms are experienced, the self will have the confidence to state, think, feel and unbendingly believe the headquarters will direct the body and mind's life giving cells in such a manner where self-inflicted ills will diminish and eventually fall to the wayside depending on effort extended of growing and/or developed will, belief, programming, pursuance and the healthy cell regrowth.

The body and mind are not split. They are one whole strongly linked entity designed all the way through to exist with self-sufficient health when naturally maintained as are the appearances of life's design. The source of design is unknown.

Only humans have fallen victims to their apparent self-chosen destiny of illness by virtue of becoming civilized, exploited and progressively modern. Only humans have suffered illnesses where the mass/ majority of wild animals, insects and smaller life hasn't. Following their ways may behoove mankind even though appearances of turning some progress around or even adjusting it seem a little bleak at present.

We humans abused that privilege of natural health and peace of mind by overpopulating, being greedy, living our lives around the buck and contaminating our food, water, and air with life shortening substances while contaminating our consciousness and spirit with adverse, undue and inappropriate guidance by the self or others.

Mankind's self-inefficiency took awhile and appearances are it hasn't changed much, if at all.

Changes "can" be made, but they will have to be accomplished by the use of updated and more intellectually grown methods, not those of which are outdated, withered and deceiving. That's another reason for these and other similar scripts. They are meant to help calm self and social unrest and instability while changing a course of self-inefficiency to one of self-efficiency.

Just as easy as world chaos and social and spiritual discontentment has slipped into our environments, we are capable of turning it all around. It won't start with leaders of nations or sects. It starts within the individual. It "will" start to turn around when all or at least most all individuals turn around in rearranging their scruples, objectives and willingness to help one another.

The power of peaceful and mass success is waiting for all individuals to develop within themselves. That will be contagious just as it is in setting an inspirational example for others to follow. Achieving a powerful direction in, of and for the mind of the individual is also waiting around the world for those who have not yet experienced it. One decision to do it and follow through is all that is required to begin and continue the momentum.

Since God is believed to be an all power of one, we individuals can also believe we are a power within.

The belief where we are all one with God may be erroneous. If that was true, then God would be responsible for world chaos and social and spiritual discontentment since God would obviously be the leader of us all in everything we do.

An ensuing contradiction would stand we as living beings would have "no" identification as individuals and wouldn't have capabilities of exercising the free will of thinking, feeling and making decisions separately from that director of every move made.

A more valid, rational and logical concept and possibly consensus may indicate, since chaos has overwhelming evidence of being humanly instigated where the sum/total of all the people are the responsible culprits and not God. That lets God off the hook and possibly the whole conventional concept of the term God thereby allowing more individual power and strength of accepting more responsibility to grow and manifest one's self for better results of directing one's self.

When everyone follows, the world of chaos etc. will have a better chance of turning around to one of peace, strength and self-security. That security allows one to realize what are the "most" meaningful "things" in life that one would really desire. Everyone in the world has always wanted peace. There is a staggeringly lot of potential power in wanting peace for a better world of people. Let us support "that" movement; all of us.

Very few people of world societies are accepted and recognized with open arms whose standards, morals and continuous disrespect for others linger; especially when a lack of sincerity in communicating surrounds them like auras of indifference or resistance in recognition. Aggressively taking what we want, fairly exchanging what we give and receive and not caring one way or another are auras of choice. They attract or distract.

## Chapter 4

# Living in self-harmony

A giant stride of consciousness growth is accomplished when one can arrive at an accepted manner of thinking, believing and physical functioning from parental influence while still young, then endure the following social, peer, career and religious pressure of expectations and demands as one continues to age. It can be a very confusing life with lots of questions, mixed thoughts and feelings concerning where one is headed or what one "wants" to or "should" be or do. How about the question of who one wants to be with or around?

Some people, if not many more, are very fortunate in having rational, logical, intelligent and caring guidance for a good portion of their younger lives. That inspires them so they are able to help others without a lot of lost and wasted time stumbling and making gross mistakes that eat up precious time of life.

However, education comes in many different forms and many of those forms are expressed in scripts as these by those who made piles of mistakes and continued to learn through the unguided hard knocks of life. Your author did his share.

Gaining that necessary manner of thinking, believing and physical functioning is best chosen by the self, not by depending on what others advise or expect. That manner is also best originated by a method of centering or focusing in on the desired goals, beliefs, character or state of mind and body. This is what the self can contentedly strive for. Without an ever extending horizon "to" strive for, one has nothing to center in on. Here is where the value of tuned in thinking believing and physical functioning serves a worthwhile purpose. Sure, it requires constantly asking the self which way for this and which way for that etc. Ask and you shall receive is always better than just wondering. It may be asking God. It may be asking some unknown intelligence or it may be asking the silent higher power within the self's consciousness. It doesn't really matter. Believe the answers will form in one way or another. They "will" materialize! Effort and belief gets it!

One who has matured to the point of being thoroughly confident of a self-established manner of thinking, believing and physical functioning will discover it is easier and more rewarding for headquarters to direct the self's body functioning in an efficient manner than depending on outside the body sources. Compatibility with the self will also be experienced with that thinking, believing and physical functioning.

Then, the self's thought and suggestions to heal will travel from headquarters down through into any part of the body and transform an illness out of existence faster than what mother nature would over a longer period of time. It is always better to move an illness out of the body as soon as possible so it doesn't rub negative inducing feelings into headquarters because when the healing is too slow, many times it prolongs the illness (the programming of, "Oh, how I hurt," "I'll never get over this," "I can't do anything with this ailment" or "This will take a long time to heal."). It lingers as one states it will.

All progress of physical, emotional and mental states of mind, good or not so good are perpetuated or repelled (one or the other) by the will, belief and determination of the self's headquarters of mind. Supplying the subconscious mind with best possible suggestions builds a constant supply of mental fuel that is stored for use in the subconscious ready to feed headquarters and is delegated throughout the body cells. The changes made are all a result of an efficient, effective and stable system of leadership in headquarters directing all body cells, nerves, muscle, fiber and bloodstream etc. One must practice the belief of leadership in headquarters as being the conscious and forefront of mind; the one we are aware of thinking with.

All the preceding descriptions of body "and" mind functioning are instigated by the conscious mind in a manner purposely initiated with the intention of maintaining consciousness awareness where the headquarters of the mind which is the director of the self's entity, is compatible with the self's beliefs, subsequent matter of thinking and physical functioning.

Living in self-harmony is a matter of absorbing what we can understand while reading further into the chapters. Extrapolating further on the title of this chapter will reveal an intrinsic value of those words.

Much has and will be said concerning organizational, institutional, parental, dominant and predominant influence "over" others. Well, that "is" the way it has been, the way it is now and may continue into the future for educating and unfortunately, exploiting humans and animals too.

Instinctly and egotistically, we humans have always favored searching out, probing and discovering what life and things are all about. These habits and aptitudes are being forced to change with growth and progress of time mostly by those who have gained elevated power and influence over their subordinates. These titans of social, business, slavery and religious dominance were and are educators and directors in conventional perception, but some may interpret them as egotistical and power happy charmers of control. Power gained within exceeds power over others.

The internal and ongoing side effects of formal education in academic and religious doctrine are stress, perfectionism, commitments plus side effects from them resulting in pressure of a firmly structured existence or career of what is continually expected by others. It's not particularly bad or good. It may boost the ego and pocket book, but also may prevent pure harmony within the self.

Another side effect of similarly mentioned doctrines occurs even with more pressure and competition where serious and dominating exploitation is applied. This is where there is little harmony experienced within the selves of the power happy and dominators at any level. Many times, they "force" their subordinates to play the part of being enthusiastically happy. That's true and rude brainwashing.

The pits of all this domination (even in marriage) amounts to slavery of the mind; old time or modern, it's all about the same. The question is which is worse, exploitation or slavery? They both experience little self-harmony. The exploited effects are a contortion of miserably mixed feelings "being" something one either isn't or doesn't want to be and suffers emotional disarray.

The slave, on the other hand, cannot be happy either with rigorous and unrewarding work or duties while being dangerously detained, but where they have adjusted if at all to the slave way of life, they don't suffer the same anguish of exploitation because they have no freedom of choice to express anything to their detainers; only to themselves. An example of this was in earlier centuries of American slavery. Aside from their limits to express, the slaves adapted to their lifestyle singing and dancing with their families and a certain spirit of self-harmony did exist. Prisoners of war experienced some of that harmony within. They "had" to for survival purposes.

Regardless of what any objectives are in acquiring anything desirable, they can unfold as "okay" when one experiences a calm, focusing, confident realization where whatever may be desired is a progression of wanting to apply learned effort and being patient within.

We exist in a time when we can freely "create" harmony within that disseminates to others, prevents defensive anxiety and allows compatible relating to form thereby resulting in contagious harmony. All good things are possible with these states of consciousness. However, they must be responsibly accepted to work effectively.

So, self-harmony is that quiet and peaceful space inside which is perpetuated by what the headquarters of the mind "chooses" it to be. Harmony must be promoted by most people to maintain stability of mind and body. The harmonious self, in other more confident circumstances, can perpetuate the quest of almost anything reasonable within the design of life.

A word of caution: One "may" leap over a building, but coming down may be rough at the bottom. We like to think there are no limits, but rationally speaking, the design of life does purport some limits it seems.

The design of life is what is reasonable to be and do and what is not reasonable to be and do.

We must gain more spirit in confidence for striving in our desires, but also at the same time exercise thought in not overshooting our natural or developed limits. It all adds to our mental harmony and stability of mind.

Chapter 5

___

# Support for maximum health

Good health of body and mind is the best of anything we will ever have. Only those who have had enough experience of years passing by can appreciate that view of life. The very young want to play. When they begin to mature, they want material things and social recognition. When they have raised their families and acquired more material than they can handle, they begin plans to retire and play once again as though that was the best life had to offer. When they retire, they think travel, taking it easy and having one garage sale after another will be the best for them. By the time they have had enough of that retirement business along with older age illnesses creeping in, they have acquired enough fatigue and ills that automatically teaches them the best things in life are the absence of pain and anxiety. They experienced a little of it when they were very young, but ignored maintaining their bodies and minds until it became more of an irreversible burden when older and sometimes too late to change.

Why do city and state educational curriculum not include specific studies on one of the most important body and mind survival issues such as the chronology of health mutation? Teaching it to the young will prepare them for what is inevitably in store for them as time passes. That would be a basis for preventing the stagnation of the mind; hence preventing deterioration of the body which is so necessary for maintenance and power of the mind.

Meanwhile, books and health stores are available on vitamin supplements, exercise for health with no end to the different materials and methods of maintaining or gaining back good health and shedding or gaining pounds. There is excellent and professionally written literature on many ailments that can be managed at home and not need the attention of a doctor. Matured discretion is always advised. Also, there is plenty of knowledge available on offsetting emotional disarray and even in some cases overcoming adverse and societal influences that drags down emotional or mental sustenance.

What is not so plentiful though, is material, substantial advice or guidance on the psychology of health for preparing, living and extending life beyond that of normal years or even better; far beyond that.

Health is one thing. Good health is another. Maximum health is obviously the best we can expect and yes, expectations (which is generally an annoyance to others), in this case are fair, just and fitting because they function within the self, don't offend anyone else and can be interpreted as a reasonable growth process achievable.

There is no question about it, a lot of detail is to be learned, understood and digested into the psyche. The psychology of health isn't primarily about vitamins and exercise. It's about how the mind perceives the preparation, value and application of a health program as in your author's book entitled "Staying Alive on Planet Earth#1&2" subtitled "Psychology of health guidance for determining which avenue to take in obtaining better health for longer life."

Gathering a clear understanding of how that headquarters of mind directs all the functions of the body will also help in understanding how the mind deals with directing a disciplinary program of health participation. One must understand the whys and hows of good health procedure.

It's too much trouble you say? It's also too much trouble to suffer ailments. There is nothing better to do with one's time once in a while than to study how to prevent illness and therefore extend the pleasures of life out further as long as possible or better stated, as long as one seriously and sincerely chooses and prepares it to be.

The venture in continuously preparing for this good health and longer life will only be as good as the support it receives from the self. It can be referred to as a benefit of self-indulgence. It "is" a growth process and must be recognized and accepted as such with the constant desire to "seek out" new and better methods of approach. Older methods are okay just as older people are, but new, better and maybe even more methods will be needed to offset the process of deterioration that time won't stop.

Even desire has to be supported. Desire can also slip to the wayside with many types of fatigue and laziness. Without desire to have or do, all this health awareness education, preparing, planning projecting and practicing may not enter into the realm of reality.

Desire to proceed can also be nourished and nurtured to continue in a similar manner to that of nourishing and nurturing the headquarters of mind by methods of meditation, programming praying, self-hypnosis, emotional therapy or a number of other specialized guidance as long as they all pertain to making creative and positive suggestions so the subconscious part of the mind can sort them, store them for use and distribute the value to headquarters for practice.

Normal health is fine for a normal lifetime. Better health allows more time. Maximum health can be a rewarding surprise beyond a dream or expectation. Circles of science are agreeing, more than ever, mankind has the capability with determination to live possibly hundreds of years. That longer life requires a serious commitment.

The length of time desired for longer life will amount to the actual of maximum time lived minus a length of time when abusive health activity existed and/or time of life spent ignoring the possibility of longer life. Example: If strict health habits began at age two, a whole lifetime of strict habits would benefit one much more than if one started at age seventy. However, it's never too late to extend life out.

Rome wasn't built in a day and it "was" built for a long life. Human life is similar where we must solidly prepare and build for longer life so that life will allow us more time to gain more knowledge of how to build for more time and the cycle continues.

So, strive to constantly gather knowledge, believe and support the desire to strive for and maintain normal or maximum health with all its detail and the wayside will be bypassed.

Maximum health acquired is a continuous commitment to the cause the same as a workout in the gym or on the road. Those enthusiasts, younger and older, know that real well.

A broken down and/or deteriorated body and mind could, in most cases, have been avoided or at least altered with preventive methods of which are enormously available in books mentioned, seminars and schools to say nothing of professional guidance and methods by your author.

Reasonably healthy bodies and minds can be enhanced and improved upon by the same approach as mentioned above. In other words, there are a few legitimate reasons for not promoting better health, but with the balance, there are no excuses for ignoring or preventing much better health if one chooses to accumulate more rewards of living at its best and longest.

When one study's and practices insight from these scripts, as said by others too, the support needed will not only be derived from what the reader gathers from the scripts, but will also be derived from the self-developed entity of mind and body.

An added note to this chapter involves how to expand the self-support one needs in acquiring maximum health. It is as follows:

Learning self-support is one thing. Sharing the gathered knowledge with others can be equally meaningful and self-rewarding. If the reader is apprenticing in this mind stretching study, it will pay to share or at the risk of lecturing, get a few points over to others of what has been absorbed. It will help boost self-esteem and support the confidence needed to further the cause of creating maximum health. Then learn more and share it until reaching a comfort zone of mind. This all adds to the science of creative mind.

After awhile and this pertains to the more advanced minds of health consciousness, it won't be necessary to share unless personally desired to do so because the individual will be sufficiently self-supported as a way of life. After all, this "is" all about support for the self, not others.

Obtaining, retaining and maintaining good health is a total of a number of assisting contributions from the self. This is what one must search out and apply to help "get" as much as one wants out of this life along with a strong mind.

Whatever the purpose or goals of life may be or are, the best health one can have will equally contribute to the best quality and/or value of those purposes or goals. One will understand more of that statement when and/or if that one reaches an older age with a clear mind looking back on certain experiences. Good health is primary above anything.

Chapter 6

# Maintaining normal energy or better

Everyone has been given a body and a mind for directing that body and energy to live a body life! That's the obviously normal design of life. It was all very simple back in the earlier days of mankind. All they had to do was eat, pee, poop, sleep and procreate, basically. That was all natural. Now, everything else is mechanized, stereotyped, contaminated, deceiving, unreal, bought, sold, stolen, fought for, diseased, crazy, loud, complicated and the list goes on and on.

Back in the earlier days, mankind was given energy to regulate their lives in what was a simple and much less demanding manner. True, we were also supplied with adrenaline for emergency energy which has been used involuntarily when threatened. Both those energies are still in existence, but it doesn't seem to be enough in this age of time with all the complicated requirements, expectations and demands placed on the present day societies of people.

Animals don't experience any more demands or expectations today than they did millions of years ago except for exploitation of some species as horses, mules, and elephants. Why do humans overexert thereby depleting their energies? When animals get tired, they stop. Humans use up their natural energy limits and still continue exerting.

Theoretically, we only have so many heartbeats left when born and when that number has been reached, that's it! Wearing down that ability to keep on beating certainly doesn't help for retaining long life. Wisdom, patience and setting a moderate pace extends it out.

We were given the power to utilize various energies within a normal fashion, but so many of us have run amok and escaped our natural common sense by burning our personal energies working two or three jobs, having to be super people in those jobs, in sports, social competition or excelling in any other attention getting activity to the brink of bursting. Poor sleeping patterns, improper nutrition, over indulgence in sex, alcohol, smoking and drugs etc. doesn't help either. Pushing our luck? Maybe.

Obviously, we have also been given an ability to regulate our energy levels to certain capacities, but do we know what they are? No one talks much about them except to squeeze out every ounce of energy possible for money, love, fame, position, glory or all of them. Then all those become "difficult to break" habits. There isn't enough specific relating on regulating energy for preserving life unless it has something to do with selling a product or service.

When our energies are exhausted, we automatically tap into adrenal energy. When it becomes inefficient, we are susceptible of falling victim to a number of illnesses.

Regulating our ability to maintain a reasonable or maximum degree of energy is what is needed to exist with a healthy body which is dependent upon an intelligently chosen life style by the self.

Energy isn't just muscle endurance and power. It is molecules of caloric heat units and in this case is burned in the body as fuel for functioning throughout the system. Energy exists less in some places and more in other places depending on the body condition and degree of exertion.

Knowing how energy functions in the body is certainly helpful for using common sense in regulating it, but actual regulating is only accomplished in a very few ways. One is the use of rest to restore. Two is the proper use of food. Three is the wise use of nutritional supplements and four is practicing the mentioned programming and/or praying, self-hypnosis and meditation; one or all. There will be more on this in proper order ahead.

Energy and matter are considered relative. Since the body is matter, then energy is also matter. It can be touched and delt with as a substance. It "is" inherent at birth and can be regulated as substance. This substance is treated and perpetuated by psychobiological signals in transit through the brain's neuropathways in the headquarters of the mind. The brain and its electrochemicals are also substances and are recognized as transfer agents of thought and suggestion. When the self suggests the human system to be normally healthy, the message passes throughout the body as directed while assisted and supported by firm belief. One is dependent on the other. That combined effort is positive. Jesus practiced and taught this method long ago.

The self can focus on one spot in the body and one ill symptom or on the whole body and all ill symptoms; all depending on what degree of confidence, belief and knowledgeable support is realized and applied with the energies mentioned.

The power of logical, spiritual understanding, belief and focused application in the energy of communicating within cannot be matched or exceeded for application to the human system by any other source of intelligence pertaining to and with science, medicine, psychiatry, psychology or philosophy; even a computer.

Keep and exercise the knowledge and awareness that something in the universe created us to be normal and we were given the power to rearrange certain matter of energy within to maintain that normalcy which may serve a much better cause for longer life than excelling beyond it when practiced in a conscientiously balanced program of good health.

Longer life will be a direct result of inherited tendencies, exposure to and with health practices and a continuous and reason oriented programming of regulating self energy sources. That means stay aware of body cells metabolizing (transforming) food or other consumables into energy. When these processes occur, there is friction and wear also occurring as in a car's engine. The body can only handle so much friction and wear, beside other abuses, before it eventually deteriates and dies.

However, the human body is like the engine. It can be finely tuned, nurtured, well maintained and even overhauled for long term use. This is where a finely tuned and caring mind comes in handy. That mind can issue orders to and for better maintenance of the body for a "very" lengthily period of time by regulating the energy within for preserving purposes similar to regulating the car's engine with higher quality products, parts and service. Regulating energy within the self is a matter of directing one's body to consume only nontoxic food and liquid, add enough nutrient supplements, remain calm, do not overindulge, exercise moderately and resolve social, political, religious, relationship or international problems without being emotionally "drawn" in to others' dilemmas where one might become the victim. The emphasis here is for the mind to exercise discipline in conserving body energy for use when it's necessary, not just to burn it.

When body energy is burned, it also returns and affects energy in the mind. It cycles. When it returns to the mind and drains energy out of it, the mind theoretically, will have less strength of discipline to cycle back down to the body.

All this cycling and recycling of mind and body is fairly normal in human function and not necessarily hazardous to good health unless it is ignored as though it could never break down. This recycling taxes the adrenal energy in emergencies, sports, sex, dancing and extra hard work etc.

The mind has the birthright to live life to any metabolizing heights. That's exactly what it is; the burning of life's energy. The energy per se never wears out, but the human body's cells and organs etc. do over time. This is where the headquarters of the mind can direct the course of body wear for reducing deterioration. Moderation may be the key to maintaining energy for long life which will allow more time for gathering whatever one wants including more knowledge for learning more about living better, more effectively more efficiently and subsequently much longer.

Where does the impetus, will or choice originate in the mind to trigger a decision for controlling this fine method of regulating our energy of life? Unfortunately, that's like asking not how a baby forms in the whom, but what makes it do it? How about what makes us make a decision? The religious answer to the first question would probably be God would make it happen even though that still wouldn't answer the upline question of how God would do it. A human guess on the second question is our minds are only capable of deciding on anything based on our genetic tendencies and what data our conscious minds have stored for access capabilities to decide.

"I don't know" are honest answers of little or no education or experience in the area of the question.

Mentally projecting ahead how to regulate our vital energy for maintaining proper use of that stored and restored energy may be inadequate. Listen and feel the need to be filled with more knowledge and/or experience to project and decide in the area of mind. That will reduce energy waste and errors. More mental control follows ahead.

Chapter 7

# Gaining the power of self-control

Everything in the universe, on planet Earth and more specifically within the self existing in static, limbo or moving disposition, is solidly packed molecular energy. It either remains as static matter or burns into another state of existence. That inconceivable amount of energy in the universe is activated in different areas either by what is the conventional perception of its maker or by forces and tendencies of which no other intelligence is capable of comprehending or proving; at least for now, let alone the reasoning behind it.

Coming back down to Earth and entering into the self again, the same theory of energy in the endless dimensions of space also apply to the energy within the self. We possess the power to burn or simply utilize body energies as we see fit whether they benefit or hinder us. They belong to us as individuals. We own them and control them while alive. We have no choice in that matter. We are stuck with them and the good news is we "can" control them along with our body cells which have become abnormal disease instigators at times.

Credence must be scrutized in the knowledge where all matter of existence remains as energy with the exception of thought and theory which are only measured by opinion, hypothetical calculation and guesses. That means, everything in the universe is comprised of energy; bar none. The universe's energy is either and/or activated by an unknown or specific source. We humans are also made up of energy substance. We, your author and reader, are delving into a "possibility" where one or other of those sources are controlling our existence along with the ongoing belief we living beings control our state of mind and movements.

Since all three of the mentioned sources exist in a realm of only possibility, the assumption of "truth" only lies within the discretion of the self; at present anyway.

Our conscious perception may indicate our mind independently controls our entity which is a state of accepting responsibility for the self or where a master of the universe controls us which is more of a religious view.

These views are only vague possibilities because they have only been contrived by mankind. It is the human contention where both the first and second beliefs or theories apply. The first and second views have been ongoing for thousands of years and reasonably accepted in spite of all the contradictions, hypocracy and world turmoil. The third view is like putting the first and second views into a container along with the last view of accepting responsibility and shaking them with the hope they will become an average and work together as it has been stated, "just in case we are wrong."

However the three views together are described or emulated, it is three clashing views and that rarely works whether it is three people, three businesses, three nations, three political or religious philosophies or three wild cats in a bag attempting to have control over all of them.

Whichever belief is chosen for controlling the self, the self must understand and accept the headquarters of mind is instrumental in directing body functioning. Whatever drive or source is up line or behind the impetus to control the mind and body, vocal suggestions directed to the body's system of cells will respond as a result of what has been developed in technique, belief, assertion and procedure learned and profusely applied.

Sounds like an awful lot to deal with, but the potential of mind with reason and strong desire, "can" promote a meaningful improvement. Practicing what is learned and developed increases stability and prevents one from becoming narrow mindedly set in one's ways which very few others appreciate. This author suggests we control what we develop within.

The suggestion to act is where one realizes there is an existing problem and decides to act on it in the learned manner described throughout these pages. It is practiced with the confidence programming, praying, meditating, self-hypnotizing or any other sincere method of suggestion from the conscious headquarters of mind. Again, more on this as we move forward.

The idea for venturing into all this mind work is to use the body cell's mental energy to prevent healthy body cells, which are totally important for our protoplasmic stability of life, from becoming vulnerable to dominating, distending, weakening and/or adversely disseminating body cell incubation that causes illness.

The mind and body's physiological and psychological treatments of diseases inflicted from outside the body sources will not be articulated on in this book for reasons of very complex, even more debatable and controversial nature.

Self-inflicted, in these texts, doesn't necessarily mean illness or disease purposely instigated and cultured in the body's system. It just means it's an illness or disease that stems either from inherent tendencies that can be partially genetic and partially resulting from family influence such as the family's cultural habits of poor diet, poor or no exercise, stress, dismaying conversation, lies, cheating of different natures or from personal abuse as smoking, drinking, using drugs, being a workaholic and more.

Self-inflicted also means that which could have been avoided with proper education on how to handle preventive practices. Personal responsibility or irresponsibility are determining factors in falling victim to self-inflicting illness or preventing it.

Suggestions as "I always get sick," "I have this weakness" or "I'll catch cold in a draft" etc. are programs adding significant influence toward achieving degrees of self-inflicted illness or disease. It's all instigated within the self.

Further description of where self-inflicted illness or disease originates is from the allowed programming of the mind's headquarters which adds toward abusive consumption, poor personal hygiene and that which instigates emotional disarray along with so many other deteriorating influences to mention.

The self, however, "can" further develop an ability to prevent, lessen or stop self-inflicted problems within by purposely and assertively gaining new insight and accepting a change in approach, attitude and necessary programming.

One can adopt a program to vocally state once or more a day, "I desire to constantly realize everything is energy and with that in mind, I have complete control over "my" energy which is "my" body and mind and my energy headquarters "can" and "will" prevent, lesson and/or stop any self-inflicted disease which is detrimental to my existence or contentment." It "can" or "will" depending on what strength, will, determination and belief is applied.

Power control of the self is gained in many ways such as gaining and utilizing a purposely developed belief system preferably through the responsibility of the self, a planned and developed program of directing the self, plus sharing this knowledge with others and furthering the cause as teaching the aspects and benefits of self-sufficiency derived from these texts.

Self-control doesn't exist just because one suddenly says, "I am in control of myself" any more than when one suffers subconscious actions of ongoing fears and says, "I'm not scared of anything." Steady effort and practice gets it.

Granted, some people do have a substantial background of developed, circumstantial and fear resistant makeup for presenting themselves and surviving in a self-sufficient and self-controlling manner or at least, it appears that way. Some movie stars can also be judged as "having it all" by how they appear and "act." Many times acting a part increases confidence.

Self-control evaluated by others than the self can be erroneous because outward perception of another person than the self is a view of that other person's act. Only the other person knows what "real" control exists inside.

Jack says, "How are you today?" Mary says, "I'm fine." All appears normal. Jack was nervous and hesitant in his question to Mary. Both recently met. Mary had her problems and responded with her conventional coverup. Self-control? Sure, but it wasn't what either one of them really felt or wanted to say. "Developed" self-control would have allowed both of them to relate in a meaningfully communicative manner. Self-control, as a result of its purposely programmed data, would have allowed the confidence that prevented fear, inhibition or intimidation to occur.

Acquiring self-control evolves a state of confidence. Confidence becomes a teacher of invention which stimulates verbal exchanges in conversation. Of course everyone doesn't talk to everyone all the time, but let's say Jack and Mary "were" more developed in self-control. He might say, "Good to see you Mary" instead of the usual, common and standard method of verbal connecting. She might respond with, "Hi, after a hard day, it's a pleasure to see you Jack." Jack might say, "I see we have something in common with the pressures of the day. What caused yours?" After those very few words were spoken, they both realized they had comfortable confidence in their relating with one another. That realization inspired more of the same and creative conversation ensued.

Chapter 8

# The cost and rewards of destiny

Appearances are where people want to know what will happen before it happens. Many predictions have been made over the years and there are many followers of those predictions almost in gullible manners who have chosen the stance to say, "I told you so." Sure, they want to know and believe ahead of time so they can psychologically "get ready" for the better or worse. True, it may just be curiosity. Whatever the reasons for wanting to know and believe, it appears somewhat instinctual if not more, where they want to know what they can reap or inherit from bestowing or staking a claim. That manner of believing isn't one hundred percent.

It's only a fifty fifty belief the same as standing on a fence and indicates a belief system only of opportunistic advantage.

We humans don't want to be left dangling without acquiring things, people, health or spiritual aspects of life. So, if that is true and pertains to one or "many" more of us, then we must meet with and achieve those gathered and strived for goals. Without goals, there is no growth to sustain abundant life. Let us "develop" our stance and confidence.

Goals are relative with desire, insight, at least some ambition, some willingness to burn mind and body energy and are a consistent attitude of supporting a belief in the self. That belief involves either accepting responsibility for impulsive or planned actions of the self or exists with a contention where a spiritual master is controlling all the actions of the self. Again, whichever one is chosen, it must serve a course of destiny where one can rely on it in a manner which is as close to absolute as possible, but not unreal.

The success of any desired action is, in one respect, only as good as the constant pursuance of that action. If one "tries" something and it doesn't unfold quickly or as expected, the tendency is to quit. Unbending belief and appropriate support behind it serves as more affective impetus in stimulating and arriving at successful goals as compared to just goals. Don't quit unless it's extremely unendurable. Some pain is normal, but let's not be gluttons for punishment either.

One of the best methods of getting good results in returns of anything is preparation, belief in the connection of that preparation with the self and the follow-up perseverance.

Rewards of any returns all have their costs; bar none and those costs are not just money and effort. They are also a matter of accepting responsibility of the self for initiating a plan according to existing knowledge and experience one has in a particular objective. That planning is purposely initiated within the conscious mind and is referred to here as self-chosen destiny. It "is" a form of gambling because we take our chances by choosing. So much choosing is gambling. The rewards fall into place as degrees of odds; all depending on preparation and self-belief initiated. These are realities that must be accepted with self-chosen destiny whether it is believed to be provocatively independent or spiritually induced. When the self chooses, the self chooses regardless of how or what is chosen. It's all about a confident decision.

The headquarters of mind can be regulated to suit the self. The costs of it all will be automatic according to efficiency and value of the effects and rewards. The more rewards there are, the more costs were paid. The less rewards there are, the less costs were paid. This is all tangible and as close to reality as it can be.

If one chooses a deity driven destiny and relinquishes self-control to that deity with the belief all will fall into place according to what the deity plans, one will only be able to exercise the power of headquarters of the mind through the grace of deity choice and guidance. That can be anything.

One human choice of destiny or another, they are both fair because of birthright option to choose.

However, the insightful and somewhat flexible precepts described in this book deals more with accepting responsibility for the self's actions and reactions relative more to and with earthly evidence and proof and not so much with strict and conventional manner of believing only.

Staying focused on the costs and rewards of self or deity controlled destiny, one "does" accept responsibility for making the decision of doing it alone or allowing another source to lead that destiny (the control of the individual's mind). It's all a psychological state of perception and is a subject to and of anyone's interrogation and/or belief. All is fair in the psychology of choosing a way or method of mind.

Accepting responsibility for one's destiny requires one to have a desire to constantly believe one sets up one's own destiny and how one presents the self to the self, others and things will be an indication of what may return to that one; good, bad, indifferent, sweet or sour.

Everything acquired inside the mind, adjacent in the body, outside the whole entity, down the street or around the world is acquirable by making a decision or maybe a few more. It all stems on how one presents oneself; body, mind or maybe both. That presentation is similar to slinging a boomerang. How one throws it out determines how and where it returns. The same applies with how one directs one's self. That's self-destiny. That's the how and way to go. What else would be more efficient than the self for the self unless the self chooses not to believe in the self or nothing else.

Destiny is a way to be or go and a result of how an individual allows it to happen. The costs can only be hypothetically determined and/or a matter of belief. One must take a stand on belief and "not" on the fence! Standing on the fence allows options, but nothing happens at all until those options are exercised. That's where the costs enter into the picture of life. Stepping into one side or the other will unveil the results of proceeding; hence, the costs of gaining some, more or no returns.

Accelerated progress of the past few decades has been wonderfully rewarding to millions of people and it has created even more progress and new wonders. That's good news of and for growing societies. True, some of this progress deals with extending efforts of squelching dictator regimes and peace threateners. The other side of all this grandiose progress is how it materialized. It wasn't just good business. It wasn't just a matter of a good day's work for a good day's pay. Most all of it occurred as a result of expending and inflaming the legal tender. As the decades pass, governments and business etc. plunge deeper in debt promoting what they claim is necessary projections in progress. While they refer to it as investments, budget allowances, sponsoring or preemptive plotting, it is still gambling which is really what one of the main subjects of life is about in practically everything we do at least in this era of time.

Yes, the costs have risen enormously; more than ever in the past and most of the costs are handled by credit allowances from other financiers for long periods of time. That's an extremely risky and painful manner of exchanging goods for barter. That's the sad or even bad side of costs for products or service.

Are the results of progress reasonably fitting and acceptable in exchange for the products and services? It's anyone's answer because almost everyone has sanctioned and supported those debts one way or another.

Costs and rewards of everything gained or lost hinges on our manner of accepting or choosing our destiny. Did we choose that route of destiny or was it instigated and promoted by a spiritual source bigger and less understood than we are?

Those are the type of questions only the individual must ponder on and make decisions for in choosing a manner of belief and procedure of direction concerning self-chosen destiny or spiritually influenced and applied destiny. These scripts support accepting responsibility of believing in, deciding for, choosing from and promoting the self and the self's ideas, thoughts, feelings and pride of self-sufficiency. Anything added must be a benefit and not an undo hindrance because that may cause unnecessary costs with no rewards.

Being "on our own" in this life means we "must" exercise our birthright abilities and gumption in pursuing what is not necessarily "true" so much as what is "real" as compared to what is "earthly" or what is cosmogonically in question. Those analysis will largely contribute toward a more efficient manner of knowing more how to understand belief and direction of destiny. Read your author's "Paradox Of Destiny Explained." It describes comprehensive and nonconventional perspective views of destiny in realistic overtones designed to inspire the reader to be a little more future conscious.

Theological views contend and support destiny of anything is controlled by a divine source with no implications of costs and rewards involved. This study suggests costs and rewards are man oriented and man creates his destiny by what he does in life.

The bottom line solution to the question of how to regulate dealing with the costs and rewards is to first understand what mental capacity one exists with at present. Next, decide what is important in this life. Last, find a purpose in this life and promote it with knowledge. Rewards of chosen destiny will follow.

Chapter 9

# An attitude of how everything is available

We all want something. Some of us want more and others want it all. There are also some who believe "you can't win" with a defeatist attitude where only others will get what they want. True, that is a little more typical with financially, socially and depressively poor people. Until they have escaped that frame of mind, they will repeatedly "feed" on negative input that perpetuates their state of mind for remaining in a have not existence. Some accept making changes. Unfortunately, it appears most do not.

Life is and must be a growth process. If one doesn't grow, in some way or other, one will wilt and deteriorate while still alive. That's no way to live. Some people grow into stagnation. Some of them grow bitter and hostile and pay a price for it. Others escape those negative tendencies and influences while realizing success builds on success. The tendency is strong to grow in some manner because it is a manifestation of any kind of life's perpetuation.

Believing one cannot have what one wants is being stuck in a rut. Those who have very little desire for anything of power and material accomplishment are usually not aware those things must occur in a process of growth like a tree and must be nourished like the soil for the roots, so they don't pursue anything that seems out of their reach and remain unrewarded. Even some of the more wealthy people become unhappy because they forget, if they ever knew, the most rewarding of everything gained occurred in the chronological journey of their endeavors. That's one of the beneficial aspects and rewards of life; the growing and acquiring whatever it may all be. When they have reached a point of being too comfortable, the growing slows down and they begin to deteriorate! Still want to be wealthy? Many "do" succeed to the very end by believing they will.

Rich, poor or in the interim, many people fall into the trap that spurs an attitude of emotional and even spiritual dejection by allowing growth to decrease or cease.

When one grows, things and glory will also appear, especially when that growth is pursued and constantly promoted by the individual. Some have "too" many things going in their lives. They developed their attitudes and desires to grow with their ideas, ideals, ambitions and careers all at first within, then shared them with others. After that, some of them discovered they acquired too much of everything and realized they didn't really need all that "stuff," people, fame and glory to live a life on planet Earth.

Being poor is a habit. Gaining more becomes a habit and having more becomes an insecurity because of the emotional "load" of having too much. When they have it all, they realize it was always there just waiting for them to reach out and grow into it all. Moderation may be enough.

This growth business is just possibly the most valuable aspect of knowledge to learn in acquiring anything to have and control in this life. It's almost the same as feeding and watering a new lawn. Instead of scorning the bare ground as ugly and going nowhere, planting and nourishing it is a personal "and" material growth of a rewarding nature that usually leads a better project of growth. That's when one becomes more enthusiastic about growing in other areas because of experiencing an exhilarating feeling of making something grow and mature. It's food for thought for more. Thinking, planning and growing pays. Laziness does nothing.

More is always available like the oceans on our earth, the gold and diamonds in the ground, the labor of men and women, wheat, potatoes and corn, junk food, advice, people, cars; all just waiting; even money. There is more now than in all history, if that's what one wants, just waiting for someone to realize it's here. It's all a matter of exercising some effort supported by a chosen belief and determination behind it whether it's good, bad or not much of anything.

So, one must nourish a constant realization of there being plenty of everything for everyone and with that realization and belief of it, one can contribute belief, skills, knowledge and materialistic attributes into and onto one's environment in an unselfish and joyous manner knowing one's desires will be realized and materialized where everything, whether obviously plentiful or not is available to be searched out and acquired as well as it is for passing onto others.

Receiving must always be appreciated within the self if not expressed to others for good character building and giving must be accomplished strictly without intention of receiving anything as a result of that giving. Giving must not be considered an investment for returns. It must be done to allow the self to feel good about the self. This is an obligatory area of self-expression because most of us have been influenced to give either because we know someone will give to us or already did. It's almost a preemptive or reciprocating obligation to make an exchange.

The other view many times, is to give as a manipulation to acquire a gain of some nature. That's open for exercising the imagination, focusing in on an objective or deciding on a moralistic or self-centered approach.

Attitude is conventionally perceived as a negligible or bad presentation of mind, but is actually a plain, ordinary and nonthreatening evaluation of how one perceives or addresses a situation. So, the term attitude is not to be necessarily used in a nonaccepting or bad context unless it is expressed in an obviously aggressive tone.

An attitude of everything being available is a perception and understanding of availability, not always resentful misunderstanding where everything may not be available.

Positive desire to understand availability adds toward positive striving in achieving the gains of whatever is available which can be anything. That's the manner of believing this book reveals. Think about it.

Unclear understanding or attitude of envy, resentment, disbelief and the like prevents one from striving and flexing toward achieving any gains of life. Whoever "doesn't" strive to grow with desires and ambitions aren't necessarily rejects or nonconformists and must be respected as existing with their unique personalities and character in their natural manner. They are simply privileging their birthrights the way they are.

Those individuals believe they are okay the way they are; at least at that point in their lives. Having more of everything is not for everyone all the time everywhere.

Can anyone have all that is practical to have? Where and when they are influenced with strict, sincere and supportive guidance or developed mental consciousness in those quests or if they have what may be referred to as a burning desire for success in general, the answer is yes. Without the strong desire or passion for success, those acquirements may not be obtained because there may be a lack of stimulus for growth. If that's the case, what value is there in possessing so much just to be bored with it or lose it? However, this is why we study the psychology of availability and understanding of why and what we want.

The no answer of having all that is practical to have only relates to the probability where everyone "won't" pursue everything even though everything "is" technically available which allows everything even "more" available for those who are willing to strive with efforts diligently and others less diligently. The remainders do nothing and they are the majority. It's all about odds for and against and those odds usually apply.

Chapter 10

# How love is experienced or shared

Love is a big part of accepting the self, accepting others, accepting a creed or spiritual belief in life or for what may unfold with time. Many circles of belief profess love is what makes the world go around as has been heard many times. The world is perpetuated around by a much more technical force in momentum than love, sorry to say, but love certainly does play a significant role in the perpetuation of feelings between people; animals and insects alike.

Love is an advanced feeling of like, generally speaking. Sure, we can fall in love immediately by passing the liking stage as risky as that may be, but it is experienced or promulgated in many ways such as falling for a rock star or character in a movie, coming in contact with a special job, city, state, car or any other passion. How about a baby orangutan? Those are all a little more superficial types of love that usually come and go with timely circumstances, but may be considered as examples of experiencing and sharing love.

That advanced feeling of liking another person or thing is sometimes very conservatively shared by those who either possess little feeling of how to share, express or transfer a real caring intention or fear unfamiliar exposure and possibly a repercussion of a past experience too painfully profound to allow a repeat and restrain their expressions.

Others who are generally uninhibited with the natural instinct to love (another person, in this case) are, fortunately, able to remain open and even vulnerable to disappointments connected with loving. They have experienced the spicy good qualities of loving and being loved to where they will never surrender those wonderful feelings and memories of present or past experiences (obviously, your author is one of them). If anything, "that's" what makes the world go around, figuratively speaking, with all its wonders and shams.

Most of the people of the world wouldn't be here if it wasn't for love and togetherness. True, there are unfortunate and unfair love type relationships which tempt the weak in spirit to never engage in love again unless it is of the noncommittal type. That can become a protective habit of resisting nature that prevents many from enjoying the most cherishing and rewarding love available beside child bearing. When fear, suspicion, mistrust and self-denial dominate, it causes one to shy away from pleasures where others are happily and contentedly experiencing it. They live under the preconceived and disillusioning impression which so many relationships exist in a negative and inevitable course of misery. That type of "attitude" in perception on love has no creative benefit to anyone and is best not shared with others. Individuals who allow themselves to escape that stance will be in a much better position to enjoy the remainder of life by getting help to offset that very negative and disenchanting state of mind. Improving their "attitude" does add toward making the world flourish with healthy growth.

The neuropathways of the mind are intermingled with places to store the knowledge of the conscious mind (what we think with) into the subconscious mind (that place which stores our knowledge and supplies our manner of acting the way we do).

We are born with the ability to love and be loved. That's normal. If and when we are fortunate, we develop those abilities to serve us well in our lives. The more love is developed, the more contagious it can spread around the world, even when there are disappointments with it. We might as well explore it and utilize it as much as possible because that kind of love is only "earthly" love and like they say about everything else on Earth, "You can't take it with you."

Loving ice cream is a little different than loving a person or a job. There is no need for respecting ice cream, but there sure is for a person, job or people.

The term love has been misunderstood, misinterpreted and used to deceive and manipulate for many centuries, if not many more. The term love no doubt does relate to giving and receiving, but also has an equally meaningful context of expression: It's a word that is perceived of only that; love. That term love describes a feeling where no other words can. It is a unique word per se completely separate from all other words. It's what motivates us to strive and feel good.

When one says, "I love you," one is using the word love to express a powerful feeling "inside" which represents how that person feels and has no physical, mental or emotional connection to the other person or thing. That feeling, if it is a feeling and not a thought, is a pure, unadulterated, open and honest expression of zest, allure and caring. Even that isn't enough to completely portray the feeling of love; all strictly within.

The experience and feeling of love stimulates the adrenal and other endocrine glands and creates emotional pressure within, especially when acutely aware of those feelings. Love and worry about it can compound that pressure to one of feeling either more caring or fatigue and confusion of "mixed" feelings. Being aware of how love is instrumental in influencing one's emotions can, by the same token, also offset that emotional influence thereby maintaining the status quo of emotional stability.

The feeling of love can also stimulate an expectation for the other person to experience the same emotions. If the other person doesn't respond in a similar manner, those mentioned glands can overreact and cause emotional or even physical agony within and can create further "negative" feeling.

That old expression, "All is fair in love and war" certainly does apply. There is no way in the world to force or manipulate when it pertains to the feeling of love. Love "occurs" as an automatic response of collective data in the mind. Most everyone has an inclination to experience love. A few do not for reasons of past influence or conditions.

Sharing love seems the same, but it isn't. One can share a life, a house, a car, money and the like. Love is within and theoretically cannot escape being within.

So, realistically and down to earth, love cannot be given or received because it is only within the self. Sure, the words can be vocally exchanged and are better if exchanged by "both" in a sincere manner and not manipulative. However, it is important to keep in mind the concept of "our love" can be deceptive. Love doesn't "jump" from one to another. Therefore, it forever remains only within the self. It is the self's love and belongs to no one else!

Accepting that reality prevents misunderstanding and emotional grief.

Words of love can also mean, "I want more of you." Even that concept indicates, "I want something from you." That's wanting to take, not even giving or receiving.

Words can be assuring and also deceiving. Probing the context and reasoning behind them can unveil a much better understanding for determining the value of these verbal and vocal exchanges of love.

The love of ice cream or a new car is unconditional because it is experienced on an ongoing and selective basis without repercussion. Sharing love doesn't work that way. Down to earth again, almost everything at least dealing with living beings, is conditional in one manner or another and must be acknowledged as such. Love is no exception. To love without strife, conflict and misunderstanding, one must first be patient with the feelings of the self and learn the function of love within. That love of another isn't like loving ice cream or a new car. Loving another is not to devour, own, direct or take from another. It is about experiencing, respecting and sharing the privilege of attraction and mutual feelings between one another.

One can state in over a thousand words what and how to love, but there are no words expressing what love "is" in the absolute sense except for the word love itself because whatever the experience is of that emotion, it can only be described as "love."

Love or loving of, for, to or with someone or something is a number one priority in life and would be best recognized and respected as such. Why? Everyone has a desire to love something or someone, even if it's just loving the basic necessities of life as breathing, eating, sleeping etc.

Love is very extensive in perception and a study in itself. Refer to your author's books "Open That Door" which is about love and "Relationships For All" is about relationships.

How love exists and how it can be deceiving or very rewarding is what one must peer into to understand fully how compatibly or distressfully it is expressed and/or shared with a person, animal, job or any objective encounter.

The feeling of an effective and confident exchange of love is one of which all living beings must not miss, that is, love in "any" respect. After all, love of some nature is the basis of procreation for family, the basis of spiritual believing and the basis for anyone or thing to be close in some way.

Love is sharing and feeling, yes. It is also addictive and possessive, but remember not to discredit those tendencies too much. They are humanistic traits and have been from as far back in history as we are aware of.

Anyone can participate in moving love around and they do when they are searching for the right person in their life or who or whatever else. Some, unfortunately, do not search long enough and stumble around with the wrong person or persons etc. That's okay and fitting though, because "everyone" has the birthright to search even if it means sharing a little misunderstanding. Life, in general, is a constant searching process just as the ants and animals etc. and they all bump heads once in awhile.

Keeping the spirit of living and appreciating life with all its differences and even heart break makes a better person and that's the strength we all need to survive. Be optimistic about the knocks of life with the knowledge there "will" be more of even better encounters. They are part of this life and they are all part of caring or not caring around the world which seems to be normal.

Love is free to acquire (believe it and it will be so) and priceless to exchange; when all one has to do is realize it, let it flow through the passageways of one's mind and become representive of the self. It isn't really so painful; plus there is no end to it and the rewards of satisfaction will automatically unfold when people are realistic.

There is nothing else better than, equal to or relative with the feeling of love except more of it.

## Chapter 11

# Manifesting and spreading good or bad spirit

Spirit, so much of the time, is believed to be a divine manner of believing in a creator of the universe, a somewhat cosmic image or a state of consciousness related to or with a soul. That all "may" be true. Spirit may also implement reason or desire for being enthusiastic with a belief, enthusiastic with love or enthusiastic with a project of some nature.

Spirit isn't limited in concept, moral adaptation, religious holiness, acceptance or condemnation. It isn't limited to how or where the mind may ascend or descend either; not at all.

Spirit is open for anyone's deliberation, especially with new turning and changing events and manners of believing, perception and opinion are concerned.

Spirit may just possibly be that which sparks the universe, all its planets and inhabitants into brimming enthusiastically with life (high spirited).

Spirit may be considered, for our measly existence on this dot in the universe, as a stimulation for getting off the fence or the couch and participating in the movement, growth and wonders of life. It can be viewed as a confident and inspiring belief much like believing in God except spirit belongs to each one of us within our own selves.

Is it necessary to know what spirit is? If that's what motivates and inspires all movement and activity, sure it is! If that's what can help us solve all our problems and give us more reason for enthusiastically accepting, activating and enjoying life, you surely bet it is! Spirit is within.

Spirit could just "be" that impetus and spark that makes life worthwhile or even "more" worthwhile.

The unfortunate aspect of it all is so many of the world's people haven't spiritually experienced and are not experiencing the full potential who have been saturating in its availability.

Yes, spirit and spirituality are relative. It's a matter of a great and confident feeling which is developed within and everyone has the inherent opportunity and ability to utilize that powerful and rewarding presence of mind by accepting responsibility to do so. The power of being responsible for the self is also inherent and the benefits of spiritual responsibility "are" available to everyone religious, partially religious or neither one.

Those who are involved in conventionally religious views on spirituality need not be too concerned or dismayed where the subject views in this book are so different or opposite of past and present beliefs basically. These views are relating to "any" spiritual belief of mind. Most everyone knows spiritual beliefs are interpreted a little differently, but must not be allowed to create friction, set mannerisms, fighting or superseding and controlling anyone's mentality. That would defeat the purpose of spirituality for peace, confidence and contentment.

Becoming too politically powerful in spirituality also defeats its purpose. We must all maintain that awareness over changes in the long haul to keep the peace among us. Let us not make a "business" out of spirituality for money only.

There is a solution for keeping the peace in any spiritual aspect such as the practices of conventional religion, metaphysical beliefs and scientific methods. Science has their spiritual striving too; such as an enthusiasm in believing almost anything can be researched, sorted out and developed. A mutual solution is simply to refrain from defeating the basic purpose of spirituality; being the stability of mind.

Spirituality is definitely not available just for conventionally religious people to experience and exercise. It is part of everyone's existence to feel and think freely in any manner that doesn't knowingly hurt anyone else because "that" also defeats the purpose of spirituality.

Spirit is that which stimulates exciting, exuberant and meaningful progress and growth which helps maintain a stable equilibrium between our state of consciousness, good or not and reality, true or not. It is also a peaceful realization where everything is connected and relative. That being the case, contentment of the mind exists alongside universal spirit which means it's available for everyone everywhere and deals only with our individual beliefs within.

If one doesn't understand how spirit is experienced or how it is grasped onto, all one has to understand is how spirit, again, is not only a conventionally religious state of consciousness, it is simply a good feeling throughout the human system; a hovering feeling of security, a guiding light in belief and a supporting enlightenment which is relied on in helping to make decisions. It's believing in the self. Religious doctrine views it as divine guidance.

Spirit is relative with all manners of belief and is what allows us to be proud, confident and contented: Opinions on what spirit is has endless views. Spirit is flexible, useful and a splendid lifetime partner which is available at anytime to anyone who either chooses to remain with their conventionally religious methods or those of whom are blending in with transforming spirituality utilizing that power within the self.

How does one develop a spiritual feeling and awareness of it? One method of accomplishing it, religious or otherwise, is by asking the question, "How does one develop a feeling of God?" Then, one proceeds to the next step. God is and always was there if and when one believes it. Sure, one can develop a "belief" where God is everywhere or only within. A feeling of God per se though, is not understood to be one of which can be "developed;" only believed. The general sense of spirit is similar, but not considered here as deity oriented.

An earlier concept of spirit was where it existed in more of a divine state of overseeing. More updated concepts reveal it is an invisible and reliable state of consciousness utilized for believing, supporting confidence, healing, communicating and boosting endurance etc. within the self or group where it is like an assuring feeling around us.

Spiritual development continues with increasing awareness where it is further realized over time by the desire to choose and practice programming and/ or praying (they are very similar), meditation or a number of other elevated states of consciousness asking and/or suggesting what one wants to be, do, have, get, give or receive. That's what is referred to in many circles of thought, as belief and practices of "setting up" an energy, aura or consciousness where it will circle around, so to speak, manifest its verbal output and return to the self as more of the same, better or worse. Until changed, it gathers volume and momentum of the same as it is perpetuated. Good or not, that spirit is or can be "developed" and believed.

Spreading good or bad spirit throughout the system of the self or among people isn't sprayed with a hose, sowed or lectured among them, it is a mental and emotional energy that definitely "travels" through the human system picking up and sending messages distributed from the subconscious mind through, back, around and into the headquarters of mind directing the suggestions and data into the "whole" human system of conscious thinking and talking. This is where thinking saying or doing is important to consider.

Negative or unpopular thoughts spoken and absorbed into the subconscious storehouse distributing those thoughts and ideas for some outwardly cause will manifest an action of an unpopular manner which means what is mentally absorbed inwardly will mentally disseminate toward others. The same theory applies with positive and popular thoughts and ideas.

Spirit cannot be seen or touched, generally, but it does exist. Spirit is real in the mind. Is it physically real? Many researchers claim almost everything is scientifically measureable because energy fills the entire universe. Why would it be any different here? Spirit, it appears, exists in static motion in the mind through very light electrical current and doesn't pass beyond the surface of the head. Science indicates the current stays inside. Extrasensory and religious beliefs claim they travel far out without evidence.

Since there is no absolute to anything, science and physics analysis require bottom line evidence and continuous testing while revealing results of research, discoveries and developments. Beliefs, opinions and unsubstantiated contentions based on wishing, hoping and sheer faith serve a cause for just that; wishing, hoping and faith.

Be prudent in nurturing a belief where spirit is either matter or divine. Matter is material which cannot trigger a spirit. Divine is belief only and not touchable. Spirit within can be strongly believed in. That's a key to our success in creative mind.

Since this theory of spirit is more hypothetical than absolute, utilizing the power of spirit within may be more fitting and applicable for everyday use, if you will.

The power, flexibility, possible deception or meaningful value of believing a lot, some or hardly any in God is evaluated and expressed in your author's book entitled "What God Is And Is Not" with comprehensive coverage on the subject, plus "Get The Spirit" which emulates more on the nature of what spirit is.

There are opinions stating anything to do with spirit or the like is all hogwash. Absolute answers to questions concerning actuality of spirit are only guesswork, so let us be as realistic as possible and not stretch the broadest sense out too far to the point of it only being an argument in believing.

Spirit or spirituality has more conscious and practical value when one chooses to believe "in" it not necessarily in a divine aspect, but in a human consciousness manner. Everyone has the right to believe spirit and God can be two separate states of existence since they are both only beliefs and not absolute material existence. The two may someday join.

This chapter on spirit does have its stronger contentions supporting and accepting responsibility for one's own destiny and belief in spirit more within the self than from any other sources for the specific objective in this book of utilizing our minds for more creative purposes than conventional theology professes or allows.

Conventional theology is not a prime study in this book. Other books cover that aspect of spirit and spirituality under the freedom to choose, think and believe as we may or under the way what they claim is the absolute and "only" way to believe.

We "all" have the birthright to choose a method of believing in spirit for whatever purpose we choose and for whatever purpose we choose for our children.

Believing in spiritual existence, which is not touchable, smelt, visual or detectible in any ordinary manner, exists as mental and emotional backing or support of one's believing system not necessarily attached with or to anything or anyone else including any worshipped entity or radical sectarianistic philosophy.

Literately speaking, a concept of spirituality can be flexible enough to serve anyone's purpose of belief, disbelief, unbelief or incredulity as long as it is only within the self.

If and when one has allowed or chosen to be spiritual regardless of the relied upon source or not, then one has the ability to make further assertive decisions of performing confident wonders first within, then outwardly. Developed spirituality can render extensive and rewarding results.

The results of making probable and overdue changes within will be noticed by the self when others taught by the self needed to make changes "appear" to have made some changes (when they really didn't). It may seem a little strange at first, but that's the way the spirit of intention, praying or programming works. The theory is to change the self and others appear changed which is nothing new. It has always been that way. It's just becoming more consciously applied as analyzing clarifies the mysteries of progress in psychology of the mind.

The course of material things, education and beliefs can and do change. The individual, though, is the only one who can make changes in the self. The belief where one can change another person is a spiritual belief, but that is deception in belief. The only one that has control over the mind is the individual. The only one who inflicts or experiences pain within the self is the self. This is also a spirit of mind. Spirit can range from good to mediocre to downright rotten depending on how the individual influences and directs it. It is still spirit perpetuating within.

Without the spirit motivating pain, ambition, lust or whatever, it would all be nonexistent and that means nothing would exist in the mind. That is somewhat theoretical and certainly not absolute by human standards of rationale, but it "is" food for thought to be considered.

Further understanding the nature of spirit requires one to realize something brings people together as one when applauding a great performance. They aren't required to do it. The same spirit exists in patriotism when attending the death of a president or with the troops coming home from war. How about the spirit of family and friends attending a graduation or even the winning of any great award.

There is also an "evil" spirit surrounding belief which is instrumental in the adverse control of genocide, torturous exploitation and other inhumane crimes among, if you will, fellow humans.

Spirit, in general, has limits with high, low, moral or immoral standards because there are no rules concerning spirituality. It's just there or not depending on how one perceives or believes. Anyone or anything can utilize or create an incarnation of or adaptation to or with any spiritual belief chosen. It's free for anyone.

The most ironic and paradoxical aspect of spiritual existence, adaptation to it and possible change of it is the fact everyone either remains the same, does some creative adaptating or makes progressive changes for the benefit of all (Dreaming? Maybe.). However, most of them will only adapt some or make significant changes based on their present state of mental, emotional and believing ability. Their tendencies are strong, right or wrong, to hang on to the way they are.

Regardless of their dispositional manners of believing, they "all" still have a choice to extend themselves in so many more directions.

Spreading the word of the lord, spreading the word of a new candidate, spreading the word of the circus coming to town or even spreading the word of a cure for a very serious disease all can be spiritually identified with. They all send stimulating thrills through the human mind; many of different symptoms, feelings and influences; again none of which can be touched, seen or sensually experienced. Hence, they are spiritually oriented.

Spirit in another sense is believing in something and somebody that has no molecular, material or biological connections with humans and yet it is firmly believed to exist without a shred of actual proof. Word of mouth is not actual proof. It's only opinion, contention and usually a result of a gullible and credulously human nature of which is tremendously widespread in the world's population.

Chapter 12

# Resolving the way and focusing on programming

The contents of these chapters are about arranging and/or rearranging one's abilities and mannerisms that will help guide one to be successful in any encounter of mental, emotional and/or physical nature that will allow one to apply or adapt to or with any situation desired by the self.

These encounters are within the self and involve achieving self-control, self-stability, self-esteem and directing the whole entity of the self through the natural and developed power of mind which becomes a gathered skill of knowledge and awareness where the mind, when accepting responsibility to do so, can create those so called miracles in a realistic, down to earth and spiritually assisted manner to say the least.

This mind awareness and activity includes overcoming various illnesses, self-inflicted disease, acquiring benefits of increased consciousness awareness for broadening the scope of mind and performing wonders and tasks beyond what may be considered normal. Those achievements also include becoming more stable to accept life more for what it is than for what was influenced or taught to us in fantasy, wishful thinking and/or exploitive manners.

Insecurity is the drive behind the perpetuation of life assisted by anxiety of one kind or another and nestles with the lust of desire that promotes procreation, love, giving, receiving and greed. No one can be specific about where or how these appetites of life originate, exist or are available, but they did and are. Generally speaking, everything is here on planet Earth for attaining even though many have chosen to think not. The state of thinking and believing everything "is" available will allow it all to "be" available. The only barrier to its possibility is the allowed and limited manner of thinking and believing.

Rearranging the thinking and believing through the newly trained headquarters of mind allows the desired and attainable to become "realistically" available.

Sure, nobody wants everything, but possessing the confidence of knowing and believing it is possible makes what one "does" want easier to attain. That's the key and that's the start of being a relative in achieving those well thought of "miracles" which are really only everyday accomplishments. No one really wants the whole world. That's an illusory, abnormally and greedy state of consciousness and doesn't creatively serve anyone's meaningful or even disruptable cause.

Creative health of mind, body, coexisting approach of belief and accomplishments within by developing it is what is needed first for progressing further with all that is wanted.

All worthwhile, flexibly moderate, healthy and growing states of consciousness are beneficially achieved with the use of programming. Praying is fine if preferred, but somewhat limited with results because the conventional sense of praying usually rely's on a spiritual source outside of the self's entity and may not unfold exactly how and when the individual requested or expected them. The individual must be in charge.

Whereas, when an individual programs the self's consciousness, the results will be equal to that of the confidence, input, belief and expectations one has in the self per se. Simply put, praying is directed to a deity and programming is directed to the self. The amount of self-responsibility accepted can result in the amount of equal gain.

Some understand self-programmed and some do not, may not or will not. Programming the mind has similarities to that of self-hypnosis. The most effective programming is exercised vocally by hearing the sound of the voice.

Beginning the program requires one to set or lie down, be still and become very relaxed emptying out as much thought, concentration and confusion as possible. A little more practice may be necessary, but don't let it interfere with furthering the programming. The program need not be a long dissertation. Ten to fifteen minutes may suffice; less when practiced. The individual's subconscious mind (the mind's storehouse of information received) will get the point as well as the conscious mind (thoughts relayed from the voice) directs it. State the suggestion of what the self desires in brief, plain and clear words of what the self can believe is reasonably possible and conclude it with for example: "This is the way it "is." This is the way it "will" be and this is the truth." It's important for the individual to state something of which can be truly believed. There is no "set" way to program the mind. It must be done in a comfortable manner. The programming is more effective when it is done on a daily or regular basis. It depends on how much passion one has for making changes additions or subtractions of consciousness and approach.

Programming the psyche for directing one's whole entity to change, improve, deduct or add to the course of self-development for more successful encounters in life is also accomplished by praying to whatever one believes whether it is addressed to a deity, to a hypothetical spirit, an unknown or whether it is to the self with a belief where a spiritual concept of God is within only. Both are profound and respected manners of addressing, working and blending with spiritual cognizance on improving one's ability to master the self in moderate degrees and comfort.

One need not feel like one "has" to become a certain and specific character of being. One's self is one's self and must "be" one's self until changes are voluntarily made to grow and set with time. One of the best things in life is just to feel good. Any changes must be for the purpose of feeling good along with the objectives strived for.

Also, striving for perfection in these objective and spiritual plights of desire may be helpful in some or many ways, but not particularly necessary or needed for those plights. Some people thrive on challenge and perfection. Others shrivel with fear when pressured. Both might discover more benefits in making some changes for more comfort and still achieve many meaningful objectives.

Besides, we may sometimes appear a little imperfect, but we are like a pretzel. A pretzel is crooked, but it is "perfectly" crooked. So that makes us "perfectly" imperfect.

Ask what the most important things in life are. One might say breathing, eating, urinating etc., loving, having good health, family, money and a lot more. Think a little more. All these achievable objectives won't happen if we don't promote the "most" important in priorities; that of staying alive, healthy and secure.

So, appearances indicate doing whatever it takes to stay alive longer will eventually allow most of our desires, dreams and objectives to materialize especially when we gear it all to reverse the aging process. That "is" achievable. That's another story. See the list of your author's books in back.

If you the reader are truly interested in being that special person within who can accomplish as much as you've ever wanted, more or less, you can by studying and jotting down notes to be compared and reviewed just as done in school. Reading the material may seem a little stressing at times with so much to store and remember, but that's only part of the understanding needed for striving with what you want. Repeating these scripts with more study, if necessary, will produce better results along with the other books from your author.

I, your author, believe solidly in self-programming and have become the person of character I have programmed over the years. It has served me well and "can" serve well for anyone. Be endlessly patient. It took a long time for past programming to become profoundly set in your psyche. The programming will take awhile for adjusting to new programming depending on desire and determination.

Never fear, when the reprogramming is steady and sincere, the results will be obviously and progressively noticed as time passes. Desire to do it, effort extended and belief supporting the cause is what gets it. Stay focused and don't allow the self to be "rattled" by the self or anyone else! Make it all a way of life and it will become much easier, desirable and rewarding.

We are what we eat, consume and practice. Eating good is purposely exercised by an obvious need and habit of which is related to a taking, receiving or sharing acquirement. Eating doesn't promote or develop. It's only there to maintain a pleasure of life regardless of what our life's activities are. We only borrow food for minutes or hours. It comes and goes and serves no other purpose except to prove whether it was or is the most beneficial food for the best quality of life or not.

Consuming, in the thinking and rationalizing sense, is an absorbing knowledge process of mind. What we absorb files into our subconscious area of mind and maintains its residency for creative use. It's accessible use is only as efficient as that knowledge is exercised and developed by added and supporting knowledge.

Purposely practicing better health sustaining habits along with gaining better mind programming allows creative mind choices.

Again, be patient with these endeavors.

Your author, Lloyd E. McIlveen unveils a chronological list of many and various book subjects presenting controversial, educational, uplifting, futuristic, self-helping, philosophical, psychological, entertaining and other stimulating concepts of which are and will be displayed with brief descriptions of each book as follows:

1. "Evaluating Outdated Beliefs" This is a report, viewed through the perception of your author of the evolutionary process and changes occurring in belief; especially in the area of religion and spirituality. This was designed for the benefit of broadening individual perception, perspective and viewing "another" plane of belief while revealing fallacies in theological indoctrination. This is an improved revision of the book's origin.

2. "Staying Alive On Planet Earth I" This is a psychology of health required to stabilize and

maintain better health for the benefit of living a much longer life. Source: A lifetime of study, problems, recoveries and many successes more in natural methods.

3. "Understanding Loss To Relieve The Anguish" Loss of anything involves many distractions and disrupting emotional disarray. Gaining greater understanding of these emotions offsets the misery of them and enhances optimism of confidence and support for emotional weakness before, at and during the time of loss.

4. "Understanding Preventing And Eliminating Cancer" presents new views on the wonders of natural methods for practical use.

5. "Paradox Of Progress Unfolding I" This is a tale told by a man "many" centuries into the future about an exciting, overwhelming and terrifying occurrence on planet Earth as a result of their wondrous progress around the

time of 2300 A.D. Hang onto your seats! #2 is a second issue later on the list.

6. "Offsetting Climate Change And Nuclear Waste Contamination" This view of the two exposes the hazards, inevitabilities and possible solutions needed now for preventing a "too late" disaster that will affect all living beings too soon.

7. "What God Is And Is Not" This is a study of spiritual possibilities designed, not particularly to remold conventional mannerisms of belief, but to open and expand perception in the most controversial subject of mankind; the subject of God and whether mankind will or won't expand that consciousness along with all progress and growth on Earth and in the universe.

8. "Kids Of The Crick" This is a story of four old fashioned country kids setting out on a weekend adventure in their countryside of tall

grass, mountains, rivers, animals, caves and strange living beings. Sometimes, they aren't sure whether it's all real or not.

9. "Paradox Of Destiny Explained" eliminates the mysteries, facades, fantasies and deceptions of how, where, way and when we do what we do and opens new possibilities for expanding, our beliefs and consciousness pertaining to this study of available options that may influence insight for growth, change or even justify present mannerisms of what may control the individual, planet Earth or the whole inverse and is not zealous, fanatic or bigoted; only assertively revealing.

10. "Paradox Of Progress Unfolding 2" This book is a continued fiction story and can be considered exemplary of "major" human changes that alienated millions of people to another planet in the future. They are led by the elements of unexpected surprises of which

is par for the course with gutsy space pioneers. The first "Paradox Of Progress Unfolding I" must be read first to understand and appreciate the disproportional attitudes and positions of people on a threshold of major change and disasters upon them. This is not only a tale of travel, trials and tribulations, it is philosophically stimulating and adds toward future insightful expansion of the human species.

11. "Staying Alive On Planet Earth 2" This is all extended version of the original psychology of health for living a longer life. More knowledge allows more life.

12. "Preventing The Doom Of Mankind" This is a stimulating, vitalizing and somewhat shocking description of how mankind is "truly" faced with extinction in the "near" future due to their own faults of progress. It's very educational and needed now to help offset that inevitability

where the odds dictate we will all perish if we don't adhere to this offsetting of which "is" possible to achieve.

13. "Spiritual Transformation Of The Fourth Millennium" Old-time conventional religion is fading. New-time spirituality is on the rise. Objective realism is the prime issue here for future inclined thinking and believing.

14. "Understanding The Science Of Creative Mind" This is a study for discovering, developing and practicing a psychological powerhouse within for conquering the unconquerable, achieving the impossible or doing things no one has done all depending on, of course, the makeup and determination of the individual. This study brings out a greater potential of the individual's abilities when taken seriously. This was compiled from a lifetime of study and experience from your author.

15. "Living to 150" is a guidance program for intentions of anyone desiring a longer than longer life which is insightfully and innovatively educational for that purpose.

16. "The Act Of Getting One's Act Together" If anyone, business or nation wants to develop their stance, priorities and position in life, this is a chance for t.hem to get their act together more than ever.

17. "Making Changes From This Point Forward" The design of this book is for the purpose of preventing repeated mistakes of unforeseen surprises due to what we weren't or aren't aware of that did, can or will happen again. It's all about gaining or rearranging change consciousness in this area.

18. "Relationships For All" This is a carefully arranged view of how relationships can function much better when initiated or guided by the experiences of many experts and your

author who have had failures and successes in their very human encounters. The experiences of more relationships result in wiser judgments and approaches to others.

19. "The We Between Us" helps us in discovering who is good for us and who is not. First it is a study in the book. Then it is a study with people of what exists in two party's minds (individuals business or nations) when first confronted. A real time saver in evaluating possible compatibility or not between the two for anyone. It works.

20. "Passion Of Dance" This is a narrative on progress, value and guidance for the dance inclined. It's informative and inspiring with its history and recent magnetism.

21. "Open That Door" to love. This book is comprehensively all about love. It's not a storybook. It clears up the differences of love

that causes misunderstanding, suspicion and deception.

22. "Get The Spirit" This book describes controversial and somewhat intertwined conventional views of spirit, spirits and spirituality. This book untangles the "usual" views and presents a more perspective manner of living with these concepts of mind.

23. "Stories Of What They Couldn't Or Wouldn't Tell" Ages are from babies to 100 years; twenty four of them.

24. "Improving On Love And Relationships" This one is two books in one. Part one "Open That Door" is a psychology of love that enhances perspective to understand and adapt to a very popular, but deceiving, repressed and ignored emotion; love. Part two covers "Relationships For All" which elaborates on origination, different types, significance, deceptions, desires, experiences,

communication, possibilities, future and guidance of relationships. It's comprehensive and also derived from a lifetime of relationship experiences and serious study.

# NOTES

# NOTES

# NOTES

# NOTES

www.ingramcontent.com/pod-product-compliance
Lightning Source LLC
Chambersburg PA
CBHW020515290526
45786CB00002B/610